W9-BLY-812

21st Century
Basic Skills
Library

YOUR HEALTHY PLATE
VEGETABLES

by Katie Marsico

Cherry Lake Publishing • Ann Arbor, Michigan

3

Published in the United States of America
by Cherry Lake Publishing
Ann Arbor, Michigan
www.cherrylakepublishing.com

Content Adviser: Theresa A. Wilson, MS, RD, LD, Baylor College
of Medicine, USDA/ARS Children's Nutrition Research Center,
Houston, Texas

Photo Credits: Cover and page 1, ©Elena Schweitzer/Shutterstock, Inc.;
page 4, ©wavebreakmedia ltd/Shutterstock, Inc.; page 6, ©Alexander
Raths/Shutterstock, Inc.; page 8, ©Yelo34/Dreamstime.com; page 10,
U.S. Department of Agriculture; page 12, ©iStockphoto.com/LydiaGoolia;
page 14, ©Monkey Business Images/Shutterstock, Inc.; page 16,
©iStockphoto.com/CharlotteLake; page 18, ©Martin Rochefor/
Dreamstime.com, page 20, ©iStockphoto.com/monkeybusinessimages.

Library of Congress Cataloging-in-Publication Data
Marsico, Katie, 1980–
   Your healthy plate. Vegetables/by Katie Marsico.
      p. cm.— (21st century basic skills library. Level 3)
   Includes bibliographical references and index.
   ISBN 978-1-61080-347-2 (lib. bdg.)—ISBN 978-1-61080-
ISBN 978-1-61080-399-1 (pbk.)
   1. Vegetables in human nutrition—Juvenile literatu
Juvenile literature. I. Title. II. Title: Vegetables. III
   TX557.M34 2012
   641.3'5—dc23

Cherry Lake Publishing would like to ackno
the work of The Partnership for 21st Centu
Please visit www.21stcenturyskills.org for r

Printed in the United States of America
Corporate Graphics Inc.
January 2012
CLSP10

TABLE OF CONTENTS

What Are Vegetables?

Do you like carrots and lettuce in your salad? Do you like to eat mashed potatoes for dinner?

These foods are **vegetables**.

Vegetables are plants or parts of plants that can be used as food.

Farmers grow many different kinds of vegetables.

Vegetables come in many colors. Broccoli and kale are dark green. Eggplants are purple.

Some vegetables such as corn and potatoes have a kind of sugar called **starch**.

People often think of beans as vegetables, too!

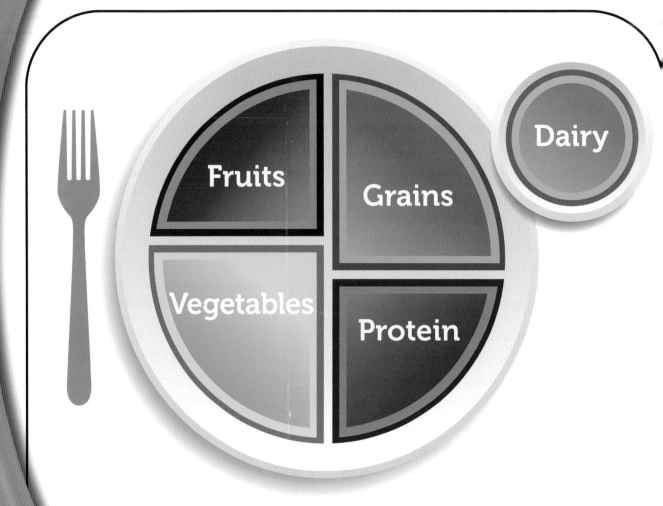

ChooseMyPlate.gov

Why Do You Need Vegetables?

Vegetables are one of five main **food groups**.

Each food group nourishes your body in a different way. Foods from all five groups are part of a **balanced diet**.

Why Else Should You Eat Vegetables?

Orange, green, and purple vegetables help keep your bones healthy.

Eating any kind of vegetable helps protect your body against **diseases**.

How Often Should You Eat Vegetables?

Someone your age should eat 1½ cups of vegetables each day.

Fruits and vegetables are very good for you, so they should make up half of your plate at every meal.

Many vegetables taste great when they are cooked.

Try eating a **serving** of spinach cooked with garlic and olive oil. You could also have some steamed peas with your next meal!

You can eat most vegetables **raw**. This is a great way to get **vitamin C**. It keeps your eyes, bones, and skin healthy.

Raw carrots and celery sticks are healthy snacks.

Think of other ways to add vegetables to your diet. Ask an adult for some ideas.

What vegetables will you eat with dinner tonight?

Find Out More

BOOK

Adams, Julia. *Vegetables*. New York: PowerKids Press, 2011.

WEB SITE

United States Department of Agriculture (USDA)—Food Groups: Vegetables

www.choosemyplate.gov/foodgroups/vegetables.html
Learn more about vegetables and how to make them part of your diet.

Glossary

balanced diet (BAL-uhntzt DYE-it) eating just the right amounts of different foods

diseases (di-ZEEZ-uhz) conditions that cause health problems

food groups (FOOD GROOPS) groups of different foods that people should have in their diets

raw (RAW) not cooked

serving (SURV-ing) a set amount of food

starch (STAHRCH) a substance found in some foods

vegetables (VEJ-tuh-buhlz) plants or plant parts that can be used as food

vitamin C (VYE-tuh-min SEE) a substance found in food that helps the body heal and stay strong

Home and School Connection

Use this list of words from the book to help your child become a better reader. Word games and writing activities can help beginning readers reinforce literacy skills.

a	colors	foods	kind	peas	that
add	come	for	kinds	people	these
adult	cooked	from	lettuce	plants	they
against	corn	fruits	like	plate	think
age	could	garlic	main	potatoes	this
all	cups	get	make	protect	to
also	dark	good	many	purple	tonight
an	day	great	mashed	raw	too
and	diet	green	meal	salad	try
are	different	groups	most	serving	up
as	dinner	grow	need	should	used
ask	diseases	half	next	skin	vegetables
at	do	have	nourishes	snacks	very
balanced	each	healthy	of	so	vitamin
be	eat	helps	often	some	way
beans	eating	how	oil	someone	ways
body	eggplants	ideas	olive	spinach	what
bones	else	in	one	starch	when
broccoli	every	is	or	steamed	why
called	eyes	it	orange	sticks	will
can	farmers	kale	other	such	with
carrots	five	keep	part	sugar	you
celery	food	keeps	parts	taste	your

Index

About the Author

Katie Marsico is an author of nonfiction books for children and young adults. She lives outside of Chicago, Illinois, with her husband and children.

24